Pinched by Memories

Written by **Ahlam Khadra**

Printed in the United States of America

First Printing, 2020

ISBN 9798680496572

Imprint: Independently published

Edited by Shauna Rae Christensen

Graphic Design by Belal Alqam

Table of Contents

PINCHED BY MEMORIES

HELD BENEATH

THAT STANDS ALONE

-Pinched by Memories-

No One Feels Me

My screams are on the inside and no one can hear me,

        but blame me

I take it out on a hookah, maybe it will calm me down . . .

        the smoke will warm my heart

Bubbling sounds will reduce my sadness.

Coals slowly burn out the tasty mint in my mouth . . .

Let the healing in -- and out, wash my body to peace.

        No one can feel me

        but the smoke spreads around like a flood of water

        my eyes quietly dazzle away in solace

        as my ears dance with the beat of the healing in and out procedure.

My hands tightly hold onto the stretchable hose in case of my fainting,

my rocking chair interrupts my calm mind . . .

        I ask, *Will I stop rocking when my heart decides to stop?*

        Will I rock to death?

The heart endures terrifying emotions

but I just ask it to allow me rest now.

We Don't Belong

What is it with life that seems not to belong?

We fly towards our goals,

yet we are not content with writing to survive,

to say what is beneath us

carry along painful spots

to our last hope,

last dignity.

We fly over the skies peering at the clear blue,

wondering . . .

what is there?

To unfold?

To explore?

To risk all that we have

for a kingdom full of love

And hope . . .

faith . . .

we pray

run

smile

struggle

cope

with the anonymous.

There is no more hope,

    we are reaching

    the last prayer

    to acceptance.

Confusions

I looked up your name to see if I could find myself

I looked again

even deeper

Trying to comprehend myself

To identify who

                really

                      am I?

Puppet

I refuse to hold onto dirt that has been covering me for a while.

I refuse to hold back the memories that abused me from the in and outside.

I want to fly to the blue sky with gloomy eyes.

I want to pour acid on the strangled tears that tortured me for years.

I want to breathe fresh air that hasn't reached my lungs for a while.

I want to floss away the dirt around me . . . it is not about freedom:

it's about love, respect.

It's about loving myself.

It's about observing myself as beautiful.

It's about being loved, held, touched with the softness of a lover's hand,

I want to be myself.

I refuse to be concealed behind a mask; nor will you find me behind a false one.

I want to hear beautiful words coming from your red heart.

I refuse to be a puppet . . .

Slow: Steady: Death

You asked me what I carried on my back:

heaviness that damaged my soul, ruined my body

My eyes

      My ears

            My "me"

I'm gone like the wind

It took me when nobody else wanted to accept me

I didn't have to fake it to be with it

I didn't have to plead and say,

    "Take me, please."

What is it with me?

Shredded in pieces each time

I thought I was moving on.

I thought that you were pulling me back to discontinue the wind

and

Tell me you need to

    Tell me something--

        Tell me anything.

I'm exhausted,

I'm damaged,

I'm dying . . .

Master and his victim

I'm tired of being tired

it's awful in this cage

trapped between charming and miserable

memories you left behind

often praising me

while haunting me.

      It's awful in this cage

      it has an undesirable smell

      a beast would love to eat me

      but when near, he'd escape without return

      and another beast would come

      and then run with no sign of disappearing.

Again

it happens

it's awful

it is within this cage

making way for an unwelcome sign

for other hungry beasts.

My master is taking care of me

showing his ugly form

he is a beast within a beast

covered with insanity

covered with ugliness

that passed a living being's limits.

Something undesirable

disguising me with ugliness.

      Open the cage

so I can release this ugly scent

let me look outside

permit me to breathe the fresh air that I was born to breathe

trapping me between memories filled with beauty.

Misery will not sprout a smile on my face.

Master, you are a beast I can't say more than that.

I fear losing my freedom.

Master, let me be myself.

I am born to breathe the natural environment

not your fabricated one.

Unexpected Approach

Pain knocked at my door,
embraced me carefully.
I didn't drop the plates in my hands.
Perplexed by its approach,
speechless I became,
searching for an escape.
Somewhere.
Away.
Away, from under a toxic roof;
it's hands left red stains in mine,
it's eyes stitched black spots on my skin,
energy was too complex to handle.
I found myself lying on a miserable floor and
heard my loud heartbeats.
I knew it was the end for me,
unable to fight back it's embrace.
I wasn't able to push it off of me,
found myself falling into a deep sleep.

Wanting More

A palace as a home, yet unsatisfied.

A car for transportation, yet unsatisfied.

A beautiful family, yet unsatisfied.

Have it better than the others yet look at the other.

Stare at the other.

Smile at the other.

Laugh at the other.

Envy the other.

Follow the other.

Stab the other.

When will unsatisfied be satisfied?

Seeking Beneath

Eyes find a quiet place,

blink a few times

until it's time to dream.

They wait for the right moment to wave goodbye to the world until tomorrow,

looking forward to happiness during their sleep.

Eyes don't want to see misery in the world,

they decide sleep is the best escape.

Eyes don't want to see hate,

they decide sleep is the right decision.

Eyes want to seal shut, never open again,

but they know it is impossible now.

As long as they see light, they will have to open up wide.

> *Soon, just soon . . .*

"Everything will be okay," one eye says to the other.

One eye surrounded with water -- the other seeks beauty.

Eyes want to sleep longer but they know they cannot.

They need to open now to see where they are heading.

Hope is out there, but they need to keep maneuvering.

They cannot see it with their naked eyes, so keep proceeding.

Cautiously, seek what's behind the hidden.

Sealing the eyes won't help for long.

It's time to walk with less tears.

It's time to open up wide, see the beauty.

Open the eyes, see what is hidden.

Widely look at the parts in front of you,

don't leave anything out.

Keep searching for meaning.

"Where are you heading?" a voice calls out.

Open your eyes clearly,

the hidden is not always seen with naked eyes.

Sleep for a moment, rest the eyes . . . until tomorrow.

Faith

Wherever I proceed,

I'm followed.

Whatever I do,

I'm watched.

Whenever I smile,

I'm cursed.

Whichever I choose,

I'm mistaken.

Every day I sit under that oak tree.

Pray to be heard.

To be saved.

I'm camouflaged by haters actions.

I still pray

I still wait

To be heard

To be saved

Don't leave me God

I'm still alive

I still have faith . . .

Can't Erase You

We used to watch a movie together every other day.

I chose my favorite.

The next, you chose yours.

      Unable to forget those moments together.

You promised to make dinner the following Thursday at six.

      I suppose you forgot.

      I suppose and I suppose.

How it tears my heart when making excuses for your absences.

I'm not feeling myself.

Trapped in your memories.

Whenever I delete a picture of you, another appears rapidly.

Your memory holds on to me whenever I decide to walk forward.

Manipulative Waves

Sounds of waves like music in my ears

Seduces me until I trust it

Holds on to me like a lover's warm embrace

Pulls me harder towards the iceberg

Whispers in my ears:

> *"I'm taking you with me,*
>
> *I don't want to hear your cries . . ."*

Expects me to stay quiet

The moment I accept its hands

It disconnects the soul from my body

> As if I had not existed.
>
> Manipulative waves, not a game.

Undiscovered Puzzles

Missing pages in my life.
        Lost puzzles that need to be discovered.
Life makes it too difficult to find an answer.
        I try to apply the image on a piece of paper,
freshly painted exactly like the one in my head.
        My brain is too exhausted to reach the answer,
        maybe my eyes will be able to find it.
Missing pieces in my life are all over the place.
        Even though I try to use a broom to collect these pieces,
        there are always several that get away;
and even a broom cannot touch all the dust on the floor.
        So how will I succeed in finding the missing pieces?
I'm exhausted from thinking too much.
There is no need to think anymore.
        I'm tired of expecting to get close tomorrow.
        When tomorrow comes, it leaves me alone,
pushes me to wander off in a quiet, dark place.
        I only see a shadow follow each of my proceeding movements.
        It's quiet and dark and I am alone.
My missing pieces are away
I have been walking for years
yet no trace of answers for these missing pages . . .

Demolish Abuse

I'm trapped deeply.
I cannot escape myself.

I try with all the guts I have to ignore myself.

I try and I try
to occupy myself for an elopement.

I hold my breath steadily to let myself sleep -- it is time to escape myself.

I have been trapped since the day of my birth.

      I'm exhausted from planning a failed escape.

      I expect to leave myself anytime now,

      go to sweet, sensational sleep, give me time to pack my stuff,

      allow me to live peacefully.

I'm splitting into pieces for your continuous comfort.

      Let me relax the way you do after a long day of work.

I'm tired of thinking, similar to the way you're tired of working so much.

Too much melts the body into dust.

What is left of me is rotting alone in a quiet desert.

As much as I call out for help, I know only disappointment.

It is time to let go of myself for a better self.

I'm alone.

I've decided to let go of toxic people.

I'm alone.

I've decided to wash out the fake lists in my life.

I'm walking where it says "proceed."

I'm stopping where there is a stop sign.

I'm breathing slowly,

in case of a panic attack.

I'm heading to a safer world.

Truth Behind Memory

Holding on to disturbing memories is like sewing an injured piece of skin on to your body.

It's painful -- it burns like a nonstop explosion in the heart.

Wash it with water to cool it down for a moment or so.

These memories haunt you in your sleep by tracing red marks on your torn skin.

It hurts, it burns, leaves you in an unstable state where the mind cannot wander off

until it takes these memories with it.

     Memories are like ghosts that sleep next to you

     (you can't live without them)

     they are stapled to your brain.

Even if you tour around on the inside you won't see anything, but you will feel it there.

It's painful, it haunts you when you're asleep, it haunts you when you're awake.

Letting go of it is like cutting off your right arm.

It's painful.

     It burns.

       It hurts.

What Happens to Us

Alarm tones disturb my sleep, yet I set it at 5 a.m. wondering if I will be able to wake up all

right.

It's 5:10, still in bed observing the ceiling above me.

How hard it is to get my eyes to open wide.

I wonder if the ceiling above is moving or my eyes are just twitching.

Blink after blink, I release a soft yawn.

My mind wants to jump out of bed and change into new clothes for a new day,

but my legs are not helping me.

My hands are moving close to my legs, pushing them to move, but they refuse.

It's 5:20, I'm still in bed listening to the sounds of chirping birds outside;

but maybe they will come and help me move from my place.

Time is passing so quickly . . . didn't notice that I missed my doctor's appointment.

Time passes while still in bed releasing my yawns of a sleepless mind.

I'm wondering if I missed a new day.

I will just wait until tomorrow. I set my alarm to 5 a.m.,

caring less about the disturbances and more about getting out of bed.

Holding Relationships

It was an enormous sink.

It was another world.

It was quiet.

It was natural.

It was real.

It was the truth.

It was the beginning.

Our beginning.

You and I.

>Had it been a month?

>A year?

>Our enormous adventure.

>You and I lived reality.

>There were no lies.

>There was no disturbance.

>There was no fabrication.

>There was much imagination.

>It was the beginning.

Our beginning.

You and I held hands for a month?

For a year?

Remember when we took a walk near the Pacific Ocean

to head to the little island behind the shore?

I remember walking, but I don't remember the island.

I remember holding your hand on a chilly afternoon,

you promised to take care of me.

I remember your hand sweating.

You needed to soak it in the salty water.

I waited for you to grab my hand and walk along with me

but you disappeared into the fog.

I wiped my eyes to clear my blurry view, but it didn't help.

It was real, you were gone.

I looked again and again, but your promise broke the moment you let my hand go.

Was it time for you to go, or was it time for me to begin anew?

I'm stuck with your memories, with your broken promise of years to come.

Nothing brought you back.

Your memories burdened my heart while waiting for your broken promise to take care of me.

That day was truly an enormous sink.

Change in One's Self

What altered me was listening to myself more than listening to others.

What changed me was the fact that you reminded me of yesterday,

when you belittled me with your assumptions.

You decided that I was horrible, so that is what I have become for you.

You placed your negative thoughts upon me, and you transformed me.

I'm not always like this, but it is what you see in me, for you chose to see it in me,

and I can't do anything but present that person.

Man-Made Mixture

Sam--

You're unpredictable.

When was the last time you looked yourself in the eye and asked

   "Who am I?"

Where were you when mom needed you?

Still hiding behind those alleys

desperately

seeking someone to buy your goods,

(at least that's what you called the powder in your pocket).

   "Sam!"

After you receive a couple of bucks in exchange for the powder,

you pass through a dumpster right back home.

Until tomorrow.

Your mom notices the difference . . .

Black bags under your eyes,

your mouth all dry.

When you speak, you do not make sense.

What's worse? Your denial.

Your wide imagination forms a smile on your face as if your content with yourself.

You're drowning.

Your color is fading away.

The way it controls your mind is unpredictable.

Mom's pain awash in your smile.

Her only child -- a victim of man-made mixture.

Thunderstorms

It's 11 p.m.-- past my bedtime.

I'm trying to tuck myself into a long, deep sleep

but the thunderstorm is not permitting me.

Creak

     Creak

It moves . . .

The lighting takes control.

I close my eyes & think of nice events that have taken place in my life.

I'm trying to calm down but the words in my head are growing louder.

I open my eyes to see if I hear anything, but I still do.

There is no difference.

I'm stuck with the thunderstorm that decided not to leave my side.

-Held Beneath-

Waiting

Oh thoughts,

you have torn me apart,

eating me while I still breathe.

You fully control my brain,

have me suffocated the moment you begin your work.

Thousands of thoughts attacking my mind all at once.

My brain is dead (it stopped working a while back).

I no longer want my abused mind to continue to think.

So leave it alone.

It has nothing to say to you.

Thoughts of being unsuccessful, unhappy, keep it all for yourself.

The brain does not want to cope with inconsistent thoughts.

   Thoughts, do you have a clue what you're doing to my mind?

Positive memories of me waking up on a bright morning

near the Amalfi Coast in Villa Rufolo

with the sound of instruments humming in my ears.

Then, suddenly, disturbed by death's approach.

Love Letter

Dear Love,

I have been drinking my own tears for years now.
Will you not say something?
I want my other half returned.
My half-heart is not breathing without it, and I don't know how long it will handle beating without it.
Love, you stole it when we were young, I was fully innocent and shy.
Now I want it back -- it is hurting me deeply, causing me to scream but nobody can hear me.
It makes me stab my own skin to stop the bleed!
Love, I'm sorry that I told you
you can't have me

forced you to steal half of my heart.
It has been eating me alive for years now.
Death burns me.

Your past lover.

Unsure

Perhaps I walk through the distance without looking back.

Perhaps I walk a hundred miles back and forth without noticing.

Maybe, I repeat the same stories,

or use the same lines of poetry.

Perhaps I yearn for the days that helped me grow.

Maybe, I want to go through my life again and rip out the pages I dislike.

Perhaps I want to fix my future by destroying my past.

However, I need my past to make up a future.

I'm lost in a world with no shame.

No fame.

No longing.

*** ***

To breathe again.

I'm healing from heartache.

But I'm going through my day without shedding a tear.

I'm just trying to live!

Reality

Doctor says I have to take care of myself:

√ Inhale and exhale deeply

√ Try not to blink when you're looking at the sun

√ Try not to open your eyes looking at the moon

√ Drink plenty of water before each meal

√ Try to exercise daily without messing up your routine

√ Wash your face when stress is at your door

Look in the mirror and repeat to yourself, "*I am gorgeous, and I am strong.*"

Release yourself from mental trappings.

It will not take long.

Before you know it, you will be in a long sleep.

Never wakening.

Until it is time for mankind to be judged.

Bones Don't Control Me

The flesh covers visible bones of mine.

Full of vexation,

they won't do what I am trying to make them do.

I move it them the right, they stumble left.

I move the left, and they curve to the right.

These bones of mine disown me.

Disregard me.

Say they don't want to be controlled by me.

They say, *I'm not a ring on your finger that can be removed whenever you decide to trash it.*

These bones of mine have been deceiving me for a long time. Always with a fight.

Now, I decide to control then because I deserve to be their master.

I own them . . . don't I?

But they fight me, leaving me hopeless.

I find myself stopping in unsafe corner alleys.

Bones have been leading me instead of me leading them.

Bones, I say, *I'm taking care of you by covering you with flesh*

that protects from the heat on a sunny day or from the cold on a chilly day.

Bones, listen to me – I can't go anywhere if you disown me.

I can't be myself! Bones, stay with me and give me my right to you.

Traditional Mothers

Mom says I cannot marry him 'cause he's too religious for me.

He will put me in a box with mice. *If* I ever walk out on him.

She also says I cannot marry an open-minded man

because he will ruin my morals and encourage me

to dance for money.

First man says: "*I'm in love with you, I will never hurt you.*"

Other man says: "*I will give you all the freedom in the world -- just marry me.*"

What is it with men and marriage? What is it with moms?

What is it with me listening to all of them?

A step toward my future isn't simple.

A step back is to drain me.

Leave me to breathe on my own. If I fall, I won't come to you for saving.

I was born alone.

I will die alone.

Let me discover the world without your lessons interrupting my thoughts.

Let me live as a free pigeon, happy alongside her lover.

Love Abused

Mai asked me if I ever fell in love.

Wait, what is love? I questioned.

Love is magical, takes you far.

Next thing you know you're up high

Flying like an eagle

Fast, furious

Heart beats nonstop

Butterflies in your tummy

Face turns red like the color of a tomato

Body shakes as if a cold day

For a moment, you'll forget your name

Your family

Your friends

Love is beautiful

but if mistreated

find another name.

A Lie

You promised to get me flowers on my birthday that coming Sunday.

The joy in my heart grew a wide smile.

The redness of my cheekbones darkened,

I longed for your flowers because they would be from you.

That Sunday came, was it nine in the morning when I opened my eyes?

I saw a vase holding bright, breath-taking flowers.

I reached to touch them

but I didn't feel anything;

I only felt tears running down my cheeks.

Suddenly my eyes became red instead of my cheekbones.

Was that supposed to happen on my birthday?

All I heard was silence.

All I saw was blank.

Nothing is there . . .

"Wake up!" I cried

No more jokes

No more man

No more love

no

more

anything

anymore.

Blurry Memory

Grandpa, you wonder why I can't come.

I see you under the sand. The rocks heated up from the sun, then cooled down

from the moon's quietness. Oh, Grandpa.

You left some kind of mark on my heart.

I can't explain how it hurts but it's growing and growing.

Grandpa, you are waiting for me to come, to give you a big smile like I used to.

      Grandpa, I took you for granted.

      I didn't realize that death would take you away from me.

I'm imagining you near your barn filling up buckets of water, feeding your precious sheep.

You look back at me walking to the gate to begin my school routine.

All I see are your hands near your mouth that murmurs something -- it is a prayer.

I wasn't strong enough to visit you before. Now I cannot wait until I do.

The next time I head to Palestine it will be for you, beside your grave.

To a Son

Happiness is when you grab my hand and kiss it.

Handing me a picture you've drawn at school.

You wanted to show your mom how much you love her.

You drew a picture of her when your teacher asked for a picture of your hero.

It is strange how my faded face changes to a glowing one.

It is all because you love me more than anyone else.

    Happiness is when you sit on my lap instead of your Spider-Man chair.

    When you feed me before you put anything in your mouth.

    Happiness is when you remind me of how much you need me.

    When you hold my hand when you're afraid.

    Happiness is hearing you laugh after a funny cartoon scene.

    Or when you play with my hair after a bedtime story.

    Happiness is when you sleep in my arms for protection.

    When you want me to walk you to school instead of taking the bus.

    Happiness is when my only hope is a better life for you.

My happiness is my own flower that I watch bloom each day of my life.

To a Daughter

I love the way you wake up beside me and tell me that you want to be like your mom.

The way you bring me a plate with a banana and tell me, *"Mom, I made you breakfast."*

The way you do anything to see my smile.

I love the way you look at me for encouragement.

The way you want me to watch Barbie movies with you.

I love the way you grab a comb and brush my hair.

The way you wipe the table by dumping the mess on the floor.

I love the way you break a glass each time you help put away the dishes.

The way you tightly hold me when you hear a dog's bark.

I love the way you grab a snail to show me that you're not afraid of anything.

The way you want me to braid your hair when you see mine is braided.

And I love the way you imitate me and hold a purse instead of a backpack.

I love the way you glow each time you move up a grade.

You are my angel.

Accept It

I wish I could touch the stars above us that seem so close to the eyes.

But, impossible to reach with the hands.

I'm exceeding the hardships of life by seeking for the largest star.

I see it suddenly shining.

Glowing.

It is calling my name.

It wants me.

Catches my attention.

I was with a group of friends who didn't bother to look above them

so I found myself walking away from them.

The stars needed me.

I walk without making a sudden stop.

I heard my name being called behind me, but I didn't bother looking back.

It wanted me.

I'm being summoned by the largest star, so, "*Why lose it*?" I say under my breath.

Hold onto it forever.

Death in a Hurry

Death is waiting for me to pick up the phone

To ask me if I am ready to go.

I take a deep breath and answer sadly, *"Call me back in two days."*

Maybe I will feel loved.

Perhaps in his heart.

I don't intend to sound desperate.

I don't intend to belittle myself.

All I want is a home filled with red roses.

Conquering the daisy scent, scraping my body from the inside and out.

I thought I deserved it.

When all I did was give him my everything.

        But

        at the end of the story,

        he left me with a body lacking a heart.

        Not needing to beat anymore

        since I'm dead, now!

Sleep Now

I will now put myself in an easy sleep.

                Surrender for what is to come.

Soon, just soon, it will be all right my child.

I'm not vain but too conceited to notice.

                I'm too proud to say I give up.

I'm vain but too obnoxious to realize it.

                I'm hurt but too powerful to confess it.

I'm shot with envious eyes but too careless to care.

                I'm only being myself when I'm with you.

Child, I'm weak but I'm too strong to admit it.

Child, walk away so my vanity doesn't ruin you.

                I'm a destroyer following my own tracks.

                Walk away.

                I will go on with an easy sleep

                until life decides to take my soul.

Get Rid of Forever-Pain

It all began in one year.
           It happened from a smile that led to a phone call lasting an hour or so.
Possibly expecting a love affair.
           Guess it was more than that.
Lasted for a lifetime.
All because of that white party held by the parents who loved both.

I sit one morning contemplating my own future with him -- *what is it I lack*?
Self-respect or confidence?
His visibility covered me with pain.
Agony left me in a cell inside four walls
all black.
           As if a graveyard.
           In my own graveyard.

He laughs when I'm trying to scratch my pain away.
I ask myself:
           how can I eliminate the pain if the creator of pain Himself lives with me?

Not Listening

Leave me alone.

I'm exhausted of repeating the same damn thing over and over again.

I'm wasting my time. My breath.

Waiting for you to fix yourself.

You don't say anything back to me

Your silence pushes me to do things I'm not used to doing.

I'm losing my pride waiting patiently for you to admit that you need me.

You are not responding to me

What I do next is search for a poem that may provide me with the answer to this concealment.

I cannot repair broken glass.

I don't have the energy

that I did once before.

Seek the Dead!

I feel lonely each time I think of the day that you held my hand and wrote me a song.

Was it once or twice you wanted to please me or tease me?

With love.

I miss us.

  Where are you?

I'm searching and looking.

I need to hear your voice.

I feel weak without your song.

  Whenever I want to get close to you, I listen to the song "My Wife"

  Because I want to feel you in me and safe inside my heart.

  Where are you

  When I need you?

  Where are you

  When I want you?

Talk to me.

If you ever read this . . .

Just say hi. That's all I want.

I'm exhausted.

I need the respect that I deserve.

I need the love that I deserve.

  I need *me* back!

I feel lost and broken without you.

I have no wings to fly towards you.

I have no ears to listen to your music anymore.

No eyes to see your beautiful face again.

I am missing me.

      I am missing you and me.

Abused

My body cried, yet my eyes did not.

I'm burned by words thrown on my face.

The moment I looked for sanctuary was the moment I destroyed myself.

Was I the reason for hanging myself on the ceiling

against the side of the fan in my bedroom 'cause you decided to leave me?

      Was I the reason for you to turn your back on me when I needed you?

      "Was I, was I, was I . . ." I continued to ask my spirit

My body blamed me for damaging my soul with my own bare hands.

      Wait, my own hands!

I didn't ask him to kill me because he wouldn't do it.

He knew leaving me would end up tarnishing my inner self, without using his own hands.

"Do it Sofie. You can get rid of yourself. You are worthless now."

That *is* what he thought, though . . .

Deceives

Their pictures on social media are all about love.

Their love is consistent.

Their love is precious.

Their hands are touching all the damn time.

        Although, the viewers never understand that pictures can deceive.

        There is a story behind every fake smile.

            On her face.

            On his face.

The truth is . . .

Their hands are not touching.

Although they are under the same roof.

Watching T.V. in separate rooms.

Eating dinner at separate tables.

Sleeping in different rooms.

Their cellphones never leave their sides.

Cure an Aching Heart

Shine my way home to cure my aching red thing.

It feels empty.

I can't help it more than hurt it.

Whenever I walk forward, I get pulled by the waves of the ocean.

The wind is also pulling me.

The trees are in my way.

Where is home already?

I want to be in my own space.

Why is home not on my way?

The darkness is growing and spreading.

There is not one star above me.

The moon has already left.

Where is home already?

Oh darkness, show me the way home.

Comfort my aching heart.

It has been afraid since you permitted darkness to stalk it.

Show me the way to cure my aching red thing.

Two Best Friends

I'm defeated by my heart.

I loved her when my own friend loved her.

I wanted her.

I really did, but he wanted her as well.

I fought for her and so did, he.

I wiped her tears when she cried and so did, he.

I held her hand with respect and inspiration and so did, he.

I looked at her the way, he looked.

I didn't notice she left us both until a letter came for us, both.

> *"You are friends, so take care of it. I won't be between you*
> *so I will never choose. I love you both, but I don't want to lose one of you.*
> *You are both my friends, not one is a lover. Sorry,*
> *but you both don't deserve, me."*

I wiped my falling tears and so did, he.

I lost her for being selfish and so did, he.

I looked at her with anger and so did, he.

He walked out of my life the day she did.

I no longer have either of you in my life – I lost my best friend and I lost, her.

I'm exhausted of thinking about how empty, I am.

I have been shrieking due to heartbreak.

I'm exhausted!

First Heartbeat

Your first love is never forgotten.

Never broken.

Never healed.

Your heart is aching for her.

Pleading to come back.

For a coincidence.

For a day with her.

Each second is not enough for you.

Your seeking not another woman, but her.

> Why would you begin a new life when a woman
>
> gave you her everything from the day she met you?

You did not know it would end this way.

Or did you force yourself to be with another?

Your brain is only revolving around her image.

You say her name when you sleep.

Imagine your first love still lurking for you.

Still wanting you.

Still seeking you . . .

Maturity

After years of becoming the woman you dreamed of

fate brings you back to see the one who bullied you.

It's funny how quickly you forgave her by erasing the ugly memories to begin new ones.

The shock wasn't about the forgiving, it was about how she ignored you 14 years ago.

You ask yourself if you were a problem to others,

but there is no answer out there.

The pureness in you knew that you had never harmed her -- rather, cared.

She illustrated you as garbage that needed to be disposed anytime her mood said so.

That was 14 years ago. You should have seen

the look on her face when she observed everyone around you.

Teasing you … they were her puppets.

She taught them well … thought she was a great leader when she bullied you.

It was 14 years ago … pierced a knife in you … made you a heartless person,

but you forgave her anyways.

You saw her just yesterday walking past you as if you were a bug.

You wanted to say hi, but you were silenced by her past cruelty.

Yesterday was the day you learned some minds never sprout.

Don't Hug Depression

Walk with me along the shore.

    Smell the fresh breeze.

Look around, there are lots like you.

    Don't allow depression to eat you alive.

Once it smells your anxiety

    it will hold on tightly like a son's attachment to his mother.

Trust me, you will melt bit by bit.

    You won't recognize yourself anymore.

Look around bro, there are many like you.

    Some are lucky to fight back while others are defeated.

Don't let depression smell you.

Walk with your head up.

Don't think about tomorrow -- it's not today.

Don't think about yesterday -- it's dead.

    Enjoy the fresh breeze.

    You will feel better soon.

Do not think about what hurt you.

It will just hurt you even more.

    Think about how to heal it instead.

Don't open your ears to harm.

Open them to harmony.

    Walk with me along the shore.

    Smell the fresh breeze. Look around.

    Life is maneuvering. So move forward bro.

    Walk with me along the shore and smell the fresh breeze.

Obesity

Dear Obesity,

Why do you happen to show up at difficult moments?

Obesity, you have chosen me as your representation.

Obesity, you choose the foods I eat

but I don't want you to control me on the saddest days.

Obesity.

You don't have to try to persuade me to a have burger rather than a salad.

Obesity, how you deceive me by transforming tasty foods

into a form I never thought to have.

Obesity, you jumped into my life

like shiny armor attracting me

with your delicious smell of sweets

while shaping me into your image.

Call me obese -- I have nothing to conceal from you.

Accept me or not, I have nothing to lose.

What you gave me from your tasty foods … delicious sweets … transformed me into a woman

of courage.

Keep Breathing

Tell me, what is your name man?

Tell me, what is it you hide behind the heart?

Do you feel it?

Do you control it?

Does it hurt?

Does it follow you?

Your tears. Your scars.

Deeply carved in your skin.

Bleaching it won't

erase it.

Covering it won't

delete it.

It's there in you.

As much as you want to get rid of it,

it quickly ruins you.

Shadowing your existence like a spooky ghost.

Holding on to it like your pocket wallet won't help you.

Breathe in.

Let it go.

Keep breathing.

Never Appreciated

Last night was your day.

I decided to buy you the best.

Cologne, unsure of the brand.

But I wanted the best.

A chocolate cake on the center of your table.

Your name in blue.

Your gift in a glowing silver bag.

Those were your best colors.

Should be the best

since it was your day.

You came home with a tomato face.

You saw the best, yet you gave me the worst.

You seemed unhappy with the love I planned.

It took me weeks for your big day.

With love, I designed your place with everything I had.

I put it on the center of the table.

In one minute you ruined it.

The place was no longer the best.

The gift was just nothing.

The cake was worthless.

The day was useless.

My pure face became yellowish.

I was not angry.

Nor devastated.

I was trying, but it was a waste.

I grew hurt.

Sad to see your uncommon reaction.

I closed the door, let you sleep alone.

The next morning, I woke up expecting an apology, but there was no such thing.

I gave you morning attitude, and you accused me of disrespecting your pride.

So you handed me a real hard slap,

causing me to burst out in tears and nonstop screams.

I wasted my time loving you,

waiting for you to love me back.

I left you my stuff.

I left you with the P.J.'s I had on.

My only credit card.

I left you the day after your day,

brokenhearted.

You washed me with your anger.

Now I wash your anger

with success.

Deathly Memories

The moving horror you planted in me puts me in a tank full of water.

The misery I'm holding onto is suffocating me.

I try to breathe but I'm drowning.

I have been trapping my breath for ages.

No use for it.

I'm deeply sinking with the memories you stapled on to me.

The pain is choking me.

Nobody hears.

I'm drowning in the cold, but I feel the flame burning my soft soul.

I feel my skin ripping in pieces, heading farther from my soul.

These memories you passed down to me shred me slowly.

Quietly.

Aging me quickly.

They swallow my soul without erasing memories.

They are following me.

Whenever I proceed, I'm held beneath these memories of you.

Deceased, helpless.

Pushing me to a nearby edge.

It hurts.

I thought death was a slow, painless process, but I was wrong.

I'm burning because death decided to punish me with memories I cannot escape.

War

The war between us did not last long.

He used his hands while I used my tongue.

He used his shoe while I used my heel.

He slapped while I slapped harder.

He threatened while I threatened louder.

He was unsure how long it would take for an apology.

He waited impatiently until I headed to the door.

He expected a hug, never a goodbye.

The war between him and I did not last long.

-That Stands Alone-

Just a Child

Pure as vanilla milk waiting to be sipped, you were only eight.

When one of your neighbors invited you for a hot chocolate.

It was the sweet sound of silence at a time when gentle winds touched your soft skin,

dragging you in slowly.

A lady steadily moves behind you and holds your neck in both hands.

You had a hard time catching your breath.

Your hands were too weak to push her off you.

Your heartbeat's rate went so high -- you lost your attention.

Your eyes slowly blinked saying goodbye to life.

The hardest moment for you.

You were eight when she hit you with a rock that ended your life.

Your body was dragged in the back so no one could find you.

You were buried near your school where you and your father, the day before your death,

kissed one another to begin a new day.

You were only eight when they decided to take you away.

Your pure soul rested in peace after a quick but painful tragedy.

You were just eight when they said it was your time.

You were excited to sip on that hot chocolate.

You were anxious to enter your neighbor's house.

You were smiling when you did enter,

but you weren't smiling when you brutally exited it.

You were just a child who wanted to have fun . . . thought life was all playful games.

Representation

Your silence disrupted your audience.

They waited for a clear story.

       Not a fabrication from your imagination.

       Your silence put an end to their patience.

       Yesterday you were a hero and today you are ignored.

Your silence disrupted their minds.

They wanted you to shout out the truth.

They wanted to hear it from your mouth.

They believed you were guilty, but they wanted you to prove your guilt.

       They waited patiently until your silence spilled boiled water on them.

       The flashing red eyes.

       Glowing red cheeks were their answer.

       Not everyone is the way they say they are.

Share

Trees wait for morning to be fed.

Brownish leaves wait to be replaced.

Thick branches wait to be cut and reshaped.

Mountains wait until the sun leaves for their sleep.

The moon rises so water can sleep without being disturbed.

While the sun revolves around the globe, side to side,

Along the moon and stars waiting for a signal.

When will the sun sleep so the moon can do its job,

Cooling us down from a long, hot day.

Moon knows he can't do his job without the sun's heat.

So, they decided to divide every 12 hours between them.

This is how we learned to share.

Red

When will disruption vanish for the innocent?

Will they find joy in their life?

When will they get back their homes?

Will they plant seeds of love all around?

When will they have their delicious food again?

Will their freedom be returned?

When will they sleep with their doors unlocked?

Will they color?

When will they hold hands?

Will they walk without being cautious?

When will they skip around rather than run for their lives?

Will they find peace?

Tell me, is it going to eat up all these people until it becomes quiet?

Will blood erupt like a volcano, or will it give birth to a red flood?

Will it stain the flowers and trees?

Will the color represent Palestine?

Reality of Palestine

They enter with weapons.

Strip you naked.

Fill you with blood.

Pollute you with gas canisters.

Burn out the cigarettes.

Because . . .

Scars of tears flow flow flow like the flowing of the Nahal Hadera

to the Mediterranean Sea.

Float on top of you until you cannot move.

Numb and empty you.

You're defending yourself alone!

Palestine

The land that never gave up a defense

The land that buried its own blood

The land that welcomed newcomers

The land that was mine and yours is not ours

The land that cried out for help never wiped its tears

The land that taught us to be men and women

The land that taught us to know right from wrong

The land that handled us in our worst moods

The land that occupied our minds with its enormous beauty

The land that we can't touch anymore

The land that is forcefully forbidden to us

The land that is stained in red

The land that you and I are from is taken away

The land that your great-grandparents are from has grown apart from us

The land that provided us with fresh olives is nowhere near us now

The land that taught us power and strength is lost

Land that we worship is gone.

Palestine,

Where are you?

Imprisoned Palestinians

At Fajr,

they decide to detain you

place you in an empty jar

wait to hear your cries

succeed with the target they have dreamed of

decide to take your belongings

carve your walls with symbols

coming from their tradition

play innocent while hiding their guilt

shoot and bomb your home

leave you without a family

cause the emptiness in you

empty like the jar you're in

broken into pieces

forgetting who you really are.

Gone

What is gone is gone forever.

What is damaged is damaged for good.

What are you seeking in this land?

What is different about it? What is unusual about it?

Why do you keep searching?

How do you want to wash all those stains?

Those memories are still there. Those lives are still alive.

Haunting you!

Syrian Neighborhoods

They are fighting again mom.

I can still hear them.

                                  Hurting one another

                                      constantly

I hear the bombs.

I hear the guns shooting.

                            I see blood dripping above their jaws.

I see red in their eyes.

I can still hear them.

                                    I can still see them.

Please stop them.

Soldiers Not Always Heroes

camouflaged soldiers passed by my neighborhood on a breezy Saturday morning

as they disappeared through the woods

i thought to follow them quietly

i wanted to be a soldier

all i was thinking when i reached the age of seventeen

was to be like Hercules, a warrior fighting for peace

who leaves behind footprints of love

i wanted to make my parents proud of me

to see a son as a soldier

drawing a smile upon their poor faces

the picture i had planted in my head was a soldier

not a doctor, nor a teacher

i wanted to defend my people

my loved ones

but when i followed them through the woods

along with my stallion

i heard terrifying sounds behind oak trees and saw a woman tied against a giant branch

helplessly yelling for sanctuary, but nobody heard her

Where are those soldiers?

i turn my head to the right and see a burning cabin

next to it, a crying two-year-old, and next to the child, a dead man.

i'm sure he wasn't breathing

i wanted to untie the woman, i wanted to stop the flames, i wanted to hug the child,

i wanted to wake the man from death, but i didn't know where to begin

i was frightened

i didn't have my father beside me to tell me what to do

nor my mother's advice to help me through this horror

i wanted to run after those soldiers and ask them how they passed by a family in need

i realized that they were also helpless, and i had to be myself to help them, not a soldier

Negative Thoughts

You accuse me of making up my own words to lead an empty kingdom.

I am trying to be an influential leader.

I am trying to do well and be better.

They look at me as a powerful one, yet they have no idea how hard it is to step in front.

They think I'm a supernatural figure that can't be underestimated.

        You still go on with your accusations.

        Open your eyes.

        I'm trying to walk without falling.

        Trying to hold on to my slippery tears.

I'm trying to build up muscle as a more powerful ruler in their eyes.

They look up to me so I must do well. I must offer my hand when they need it.

You still go on with your accusations that never end.

        They want me to be their leader.

        I won't fall when you want me to.

        I won't weep with devastation when you expect me to.

        I won't proceed in concealing myself.

        I don't want to be bad. I don't want to do wrong.

            I want to be good and do good things.

            I really want to.

Humiliate

They held a pistol to your head,

ordered you to strip down in front of your father.

It's time to humiliate a covered woman.

A father being modest may be a crime to others in our time.

The stripping off of clothes didn't hurt as much as watching your father

forcefully closing his eyes

holding to his tears while listening to your cries.

Injuring you in front of your father sprouted smiles on their faces.

Your misery fed them.

Their actions represented so-called "manhood". You, a woman, weak as they expected you to

be.

They thought they were men by torturing a woman like you.

They didn't realize that they were the weakest of all mankind.

You were their victim . . . you cried with all your heart.

Your last breath set your peaceful soul free. Your father next to you calmed your dying soul.

He didn't know you were already gone.

What happened here must stay here.

New Zealand Massacre

Concealed behind mask and weapon,

you hid a wicked face beneath terrible actions

on a Friday afternoon.

Imagining yourself in a video game,

you stormed in

when they were confronting God.

You thought of a plan for days.

You held a pistol in your hand.

We mourned 49 people that day.

What human celebrates lyrically with "Let's Party"

and laughs at the ongoing red stains?

With the support of your kind.

God is watching, I say.

My eyes blur the misery you planted in those mosques.

A pistol in your hand while greeted with love.

Welcome brother.

Shoot, and shoot you do.

Back and forth you proceed . . . like I don't know what to call you . . .

Esra

I cried out for help.

My own family tortured me.

I wanted someone to hold me.

Take me to another world where I was safe.

I waited for someone to open the door and push my brothers,

including my sister's husband,

off of me.

They abused me.

Bruised me all over.

I screamed desperately for my savior.

I needed someone to help me.

"Mom, give me a hand."

I wanted some relief . . . mom, it should have been you who stopped them and said,

"This is my baby, leave her alone."

Mom, you said no words.

They hurt me physically and you did it mentally.

I cried for help and you sat there.

Mom, I'm your daughter -- is that not enough to save me?

Police, doctors, someone help me, they are brutally hurting me!

I'm screaming and screaming until my voice hurts.

Mom, your own son killed me!

Mom, my dad and brothers and cousin are killing me. Mom, do something, end it!

They killed me mom.

I couldn't move anymore.

Nor cry anymore.

I couldn't scream anymore.

Your own daughter is

dead now.

Your silence -- your eyes -- destroyed me.

Bleeding Gaza

Shocks like an electric band around your neck.
The moment you hear about it
and see it with your own eyes . . .

It's in Palestine:
slow shrieks
bars all around
trapping the innocent.

This place wrinkles faces quickly.
Breaks an arm or two.
Breaks a leg or two.
Blinds people of the city.
Some become deaf.
Unable to walk from their homes.
But homes collapse on them.

Rooftops lie on top of sick bodies.
These are mourned the next few hours
by baby sons and daughters.

Some have cancer and need to see a doctor
yet can't leave their doors.
Others are starving
yet can't afford to have an apple.
Some are thirsty, but there is no water.
Others want to read, yet they can't go to school.

Some want to leave for another city, but they are not permitted to.

Deprived of comfort.
Placed in a lifetime-cage.
All must be cautious.
Observe surroundings in case of bullet attacks.
They are born crying.
Alone.
Often next to their mom's dead body
who dies quick
and alone too.
After a severe disease,
nobody wipes these tears.

Gaza is bleeding.
Don't you want to see it?

Waiting to Smile

She tells me she misses her father every time she sees me.

She tells me that her father is coming.

He plans to come for her birthday.

      She has not seen him for five years.

      She is now 10.

      She plans a welcome party for him, although *her* birthday is coming up.

      She waits for him.

When the time comes, he is in a coffin.

Not only his own, but her mother's coffin, too.

At that moment her smile breaks.

Her happiness fades away.

She lies next to them.

Sadness covers them all.

She just wanted to see her father . . . but now both parents are gone.

Innocent Family

Halloween night.
I'm strolling with dad and mom.

When I grow up, I want to be a loving father like dad.
I want to grow up with a big heart like my mom.

I want to grow up beside them.
Watch them get old together.

I want to know what it means to have a family.
      To be strong like dad.
      To be a defender like mom.

I want to watch a football game with dad.
Want to help mom bake some delicious cookies.

      But a random alcoholic took that away from us.
      Mom, dad, you were teaching me how to trick-or-treat.
      You were teaching me how to relax on a Thursday night.

I don't think you thought of dying.
I think you were enjoying the moment just strolling
the lovely neighborhood of Los Cerritos Park.

      You were thinking of helping me grow into a man.
      You wanted me to be a doctor.
      You wanted to continue to pursue your dreams.

I never knew that a drunk driver could ruin our lives.
We had a strong bond, but within minutes it was destroyed.

      Dad, you instantly died that night.
      I followed you on Saturday.
      Mom followed us Sunday.
      We are always together.

Rawan

Rawan wanted to be free
        she only needed her children
        3, 5 ,7,
        still lurking for their mother's warmth.
Rawan constantly fought against a heartless, conceited loser --
her husband. W*ell, now -- her ex.*

But she did give him a second chance at love
just to be beside her children
to watch them grow
to choose their own path
to enjoy every moment of laughter with them
her children--
she didn't want anyone else.

Her husband approached her with an invitation for a lovely date
to renew their memories together.
Her heart beat like the first day she fell in love with him
nine years ago
when they met on a random evening at a park.
Astonished with his quick transformation
she accepted his offer
in a pink floral dress.
After a soothing dinner
they headed to a hotel in Jericho.
He laughed at his own crushing decisiveness
gave himself a pat on the shoulder while holding a sharp dagger
waiting until her back was toward him
in slow, quick motion he jabbed it into her
blood dripped down her body.
She didn't have time to ask
        why?
        how?
It happened.
She didn't have the strength to move her lips
he shredded every piece of her flesh.
thrust all of her into one big bag
headed to his truck and drove 25 miles until the Dead Sea was in view
waited for a clear sight, then dumped her flesh and burning bag into the sea.

Giggled a few times.
Walked away.

He wasn't jailed.
His parents bribed her parents.
Money to bury her justice.
Accept it.
Walk away.

Her family, speechless.
Like it never happened!
Money covers pain sometimes.
According to her parents.

Damn Time

It's 4 a.m.
Armed men outside.
Loud knocking, then bust in like lunatics.
They don't look horrifying
But they hide behind their weapons.
Thunder, W*here is he?*
Nobody answers.

They begin hitting the men of the house with their pistols until blood colors the walls.
Women of the house shout:
He is not here
He is gone.
Please leave us alone!

They stop, and choose to occupy the home for some time,
separate the men from the women inside two small rooms.
They shower in the innocent's home
Observe television while waiting for their chosen prisoner to show up.
They don't have warrants, nor any crime actions recorded against him.
They only decide to take him.
Just for fun.
To grow horror in the hearts of his family and friends.

Men were hit until no longer breathing.
Women were abused until they couldn't cry.
The man did not come home.

After two long days of torture
Armed men walked out.
Commanded the home be demolished.
Continued on to the next target.
It becomes a hobby.

Death of Hamza

Hamza: Come over for dinner my friend.

Sleep over, I will take care of you my friend.

I will see you at work tomorrow and I will collect the money for pilgrimage.

I will see you later.

I am proud to have a doctor friend beside me and I am happy to be a helper for God.

I will do my best to save those in need.

I will do my best to take pregnant women straight to hospital.

I will do my best to take injured men to safety.

I will save our children.

I am a purehearted man, but I am not loud about it.

My friend, my son passed his senior finals with a high GPA.

He wants to be a doctor like you.

You are his role model, not only his but everyone's.

Doctor: You're my brother from a different mother.

I will always be there for you.

Let's go to Jordan.

I secretly call my cousin to help me murder you -- my best friend Hamza.

Well, I let you think I am your best friend.

I need to get to that money you saved from those planning to go to Saudi Arabia, but first you must disappear.

Cousin, can you help me betray Hamza?

Doctor's Cousin: Welcomes both to her apartment on a hot summer evening.

Holds the security guards with long-lasting conversations

about anything that pops in her head

just so cousin and Hamza go unnoticed.

She slowly turns off the control cameras in the whole building.

Hamza: My friend, I'm exhausted and hungry.

My friend, you drug me and when I fall into a deep sleep

you split my head

from my body, carelessly.

You cut me into three pieces.

My body becomes separated.

Your eyes full of money and greed.

You don't drop a tear.

You pour on to my dead flesh, acid,

melting me in seconds.

You put my dead self in luggage.

Take me to the nearest hiding spot.

Burn what's left of me and bury me to conceal your crime.

You walk away.

You continue your routine life as a doctor.

The image of a hero.

You go to work spitting out lies.

"He ran away with the money" and "I cannot find him."

Ruining my reputation.

Those people who dreamed of pilgrimage to Mecca couldn't go

because the money was all gone.

They head to my house

to destroy my home.

You played the victim, doctor.

You were suddenly caught.

Lies end sooner or later.

Medical Technician Killed

Oh how hard it is to mourn for your death Hamza.

Your loss poured acid in our hearts.

We melted with you the day you were slaughtered by the closest to your heart.

We don't need to know you personally to feel you.

We choked when we heard your story.

Wept when we saw your image.

Your eyes said it all.

You were a hero and always will be.

We are sorry for the worst death ever to happen on a red and white suit who owns an ambulance.

A helpless soul you were who will be rewarded in Heaven.

Hamza

Made in the USA
Columbia, SC
30 May 2024

36304498R00050